THE ODD SOCK EXCHANGE

DAVID MARK WILLIAMS

Cinnamon Press

INDEPENDENT INNOVATIVE INTERNATIONAL

Published by Cinnamon Press
Meirion House
Tanygrisiau
Blaenau Ffestiniog
Gwynedd, LL41 3SU
www.cinnamonpress.com

The right of David Mark Williams to be identified as author of this work has been asserted by him in accordance with the Copyright, Designs and Patent Act, 1988. Copyright © 2015 David Mark Williams
ISBN: 978-1-909077-85-0
British Library Cataloguing in Publication Data. A CIP record for this book can be obtained from the British Library.

Designed and typeset in Palatino by Cinnamon Press. Printed in Poland

Original cover design by Adam Craig

Cinnamon Press is represented in the UK by Inpress Ltd www.inpressbooks.co.uk and in Wales by the Welsh Books Council www.cllc.org.uk

Acknowledgements

Thanks are due to the editors of the following magazines and anthologies, who published some of these poems or earlier versions of them: *Envoi, Prole, Orbis, South, Markings, Reach, The Fankle, Southlight, Sarasvati, Ink Sweat and Tears, The Journal, The Interpreter's House,* and *three drops from a cauldron; The Infinity We Swim In* (New Zealand Poetry Society, 2007), *Losing the Edge* (Ragged Raven Press, 2009), *The World is Made of Glass* (Ragged Raven Press, 2010), *Ice Diver* (New Zealand Poetry Society, 2011), *Nothing Left to Burn* (Ragged Raven Press, 2011), *Aesthetica Creative Writing Annual* (Aesthetica Publishing, 2012), *Building a Time Machine* (New Zealand Poetry Society, 2012), *Shorelines* (New Voices Press, 2012), *Words that Signify* (Poetry Space Ltd, 2012), *Heart Shoots* (Indigo Dreams Publishing, 2013), *Nothing Recognisable as Human* (Poetry Space Ltd, 2013) and *Wherever You Roam* (Pankhearst 2015). The title poem, 'The Odd Sock Exchange', was highly commended in the NZPS International Competition 2007 and several other poems have been placed in or won competitions.

I have so many people to thank, including many whose impact has been so significant that I must name them : Jan Fortune and Pete Marshall, who were so encouraging of my work at the Tyn Y Coed writing course back in November 2012 and special thanks to Jan for believing in my writing enough to publish this collection; Kim Ayres, who got me performing poetry again; Chrys Salt and John Hudson, at the Bakehouse Arts Centre; Mavis Gulliver for her assiduous advice and help with getting the submission of *The Odd Sock Exchange* completed and for her continuing critical feedback and support ; Graham and Rae Leigh, my biggest fans, Mary Smith and Sally Hinchcliffe and all my other pals at the Dumfries Writers' Group. I'd also like to thank Donald Adamson, Elspeth Brown, Linda Martin, Mo Ray and Brian Joyce, Neil and Alison Brown, Terry and Julia Stothard; and last of all the three people who mean the most to me in the world: Val, Meredith and Mam.

Contents

In Memoriam
William David Williams 1926 – 2013

For my mother, Joan Williams

The Odd Sock Exchange

Ariel Gives up a Promising Career in Local Government

Goodbye open-plan office, my cloven pine
for too long, soul stitched into a suit of grey,
a tight collar choking my song.
Farewell filing cabinets of stifled initiative!
Tell that man in finance he was wrong.
It did not help to be mad.
Now I'm poised to go, ready for the spell
of confinement to break.
Outside the white fields are waiting.
Being the last to leave, I could open a window
and let myself fall, hitting the ground
with no more impact than a feather,
but I'll take the stairs to stretch my exit out,
weighing each step as I go down,
clothing myself in light, invisible again,
only my voice beside you, issuing wild directives
you will feel compelled to act upon.

The Odd Sock Exchange

If you're interested,
do come and visit.
Please do not be put off
by the remoteness.
If it's a fine day
we'll be sitting outside,
ready to greet you with a smile,
with no hint of derision.
Everyone is welcome
no matter how straight
or compromised you are.
It started as a jest
as you might have surmised,
a lobbed frisbee of an idea
that soared off in slow motion
over the surrounding trees,
but now the lines of punters
tumbling up are not a dream,
while inside, more socks
than you can find words for
are heaped and ready
to be scrabbled through.
So do make the effort.
We will not deceive you.
Of course, sometimes
matches fail to happen
In which case, you are welcome
to simply discard.
It's good for you to let go.
It's good for us,
renewing our supply.
We are here to help
but you must realise
we do this in our own time
for no remuneration.
Forgive us then for not
giving you our full attention.
Sometimes you might find us
a little distracted —
by a few acres of sunshine

upon a distant hill,
by an erratic breeze
through a sycamore tree,
by a swarm of gnats in sunlight,
plentiful as angels,
the piping of the lupins
in our cottage garden.
You know, that kind of thing.
We cannot allow
these moments to pass
unacknowledged.
So be patient.
It's time to end the yearning
an odd sock stirs,
to bring things to a close,
to trust that what you're looking for
is waiting for you here.

The Cloud Room

It was all you could imagine,
your home among the clouds,
that room in the sky you gave a name to.

It fitted you so well, perched at the top of the house,
the loose window frame rattling
with every gust of wind.

It was a room where you were always dreaming,
sitting at your thin desk,
writing with a lit compulsion.

Being alone was a delirious freefall
arrested only by the men who set themselves
beside you, convenient as ashtrays.

Every evening you would begin
tracing a spine of cirrus with the pills you took
to wrap yourself in cotton wool.

You liked those slow evenings best
when twilight would fall like dust,
the city stripped down to a web of lights.

And in sleep, sometimes you rolled from bed
to fly away, swimming through the air,
silent and blind as a cloud.

The Year of my First Wedding

During the springtime of that year,
the war began: two syllables of triumph
crowing from a front page,
a grainy shot of a dissolving ship.

While we walked in the park
through shaken petals of white blossom,
men fell, on fire, into a dark sea.

Drink Argentina Dry, an off-licence slogan ran,
and a small army of drinkers
responded to the call, carrying home
their bottles of wine like unexploded bombs,
as though wading waist deep in water.

The week before the big day, I left a hole
in the lounge where I should have been,
witnessing an incursion of early presents.
The crinkling of all that paper had set me off.

The day of the wedding rumbled into place.
It had been prepared so beautifully, a sky
of powdered blue hoisted as far as it would go,
with the sun bright enough to burn us.
All the photographs show our eyes
hard pressed to keep from closing.

The night before I listened to my heart
drum its reservations, rasping through
the coiled springs of the folding bed,
until I awoke into the lucid dream
of going through with it.

After that, the speeches were a breeze.
When the best man read out the telegram
from Galtieri, defiant still, there was a ripple of unease
quickly turning into a chorus of jeers
as though everyone agreed, and it had to be said,
we had indeed fought a good war there.

John Dryden's Jackdaws

He has tried so many times to shut them out
but they keep shadowing him,
strutting and brooding at the edges
of his perfectly composed world,
these creatures of fate and mayhem,
spirits of havoc, firing their hoarse alarms,
tracing the silver courses of a breeze
through the unruly grass, punctuating dark dreams
with the white points of their eyes.

This morning he can hear them again,
all through the service, jabbering
and jeering on the sills of the belfry.

What they ignite in his mind is a scene
of a hot desert land where a sphinx of quartz
looms through air that ripples and bends,
overriding the worthy but interminable sermon
as much as the constant ache of his fundament
no amount of discreet adjustment can allay.

All he needs, he recalls, is to focus,
to catch the perfected notes of the spheres
that these birds so sorely disrupt,
to measure out each well tempered syllable,
to garner the odd sparkling conceit.

Why then does an impulse possess him
to jump up and rush clattering down the aisle
into the sunshine, to tear off his wig
and hurl it like a clod of earth into the air?

All the while he knows God's white eye,
like a bright moon, is probing the souls
of everyone gathered here. But he is not afraid.
He can be trusted to patrol his own heart,
to set forth all his works with an easy mind,
each gilded vessel gliding sedately
over unruffled seas, and of jackdaws
there will be no mention.

The Day of the Slow Driver

The day is near, when they will outnumber us.
In convoys of sedate progress, they will rein us in,
possessing all roads, all motorway lanes.

We will soften, we will change our ways,
the heedless ones, the speed fiends,
the rabid dogs of the road,
even those who keep their headlights blazing
on the brightest of days to proclaim
that behind you is a driver who likes to drive hard.

They are here to save us from ourselves
so that we may embrace a gentler world
and begin to notice what we have been missing
all this time: when it is the meadowsweet blows
or the autumn tints are showing again,
how more and more oystercatchers have taken
to feeding inland and we will as a matter of course
grind to a halt to allow all pheasants
time to dither their way to safety.

We will have no choice but to fall in line,
compelled never to drive without some form of headgear,
blithe and frankly quite puzzled, should the law
ever pull us over. All the days thereafter
will be the same as we begin to forget how it was
to burn the road, to roar off into the void.

The Devil's School of Motoring

It's all to do with style.
Be cool and the rest will follow.
Keep your eyes hidden behind shades
at all times and if you smile
always ensure you do so sardonically.
Listen to that bass line,
smacking out a twisted heartbeat.
Be guided by that. When you drive,
drive like Harpo Marx partied,
like Mozart whipped an orchestra into a frenzy.
What I'm saying is, drive as though
you damn well mean it.
You're a sensitive driver, I can see.
You drive like a poet but on these roads,
the direction we're going,
I want more of a demon.
Without my narrative to guide you,
you're still going to pieces.
That last manoeuvre even had me scared!
You were fine for a time,
but when we got to the roundabout, it has to be said,
the arse dropped out of the bucket.
Remember. Keep that head moving!
Give me a full 360 degrees.
I would guess you are a clever man
though I don't mean that as a compliment.
I've had farm boys thick as two short planks
take to this like ducks to water.
We've got a problem here
but it's not insurmountable so don't be discouraged.
Do as I say and you'll do well
though I fear you're going to need
an awful lot more lessons.

Dust

Those moments in a sun filled room,
when you notice a cloud of dust
constellating the air,

show you what breath is,
how finely adulterated,

a mood of gathering twilight
dissolving through you in a slow fugue,
a movement that goes on forever.

Where you are is always the centre of it,
held now in a trance, a reverie
by these falling monosyllables,
of which you too are composed.

But the grey patina that forms
softening where it settles,
you itch to brush away

as if it were enough,
another thing done,
to remove that trace of how you shone,
how you caught the light.

Wall of Death

This machine has a heart welded to my own,
the chrome bones my folded wings.

The sky's a drum of blue today.
The clouds are whipped flags blown free.

Another rolled-up audience is looking down,
their pumpkin heads placed above the rim.

Soon I will rattle their faces into a blur.
I will break the sky to pieces, load the air

with the scent of burning oil,
and riding on thunder, circle the abyss.

Whatever they want to see is of no concern to me.
This wall of death is all I live for.

What's left is gravity, too much to hold in place,
too much that's fragile, that might fall.

Carson McCullers Overcomes
her Agoraphobia by Consenting
to be Carried

Her constant yes to everything
sets in motion days that skitter away like dreams.

This man for instance
standing at the foot of her bed.
She does not know him or where he has come from.

He claims they have an arrangement.
He is hungry for the lunch they planned to share.
That is all very well, but she has to confess,
it is beyond her to step outside today.

The streets of Paris are too broad.
There are not enough rivets to hold the sky in place.

What then if she were to consent
to be carried in his arms to a restaurant nearby.

Yes, she replies,
promising to make herself as light as possible.

When he hoists her up, he is surprised
to find she has more substance
than he had thought, that she is not weightless,
has contours, pads of soft flesh.

She keeps her head buried as they move
so she will not have to suffer anyone's scrutiny.

He will carry her forever,
his chest tattooed with her signature,
a small fir tree, an almond shaped eye.

Counting

I count things, he tells me.
Now and again, when the mood takes him.
Not so much to pass the time
but to keep his brain oiled and warm.
Think of it as a car you rarely drive.
It's a good idea to turn the engine on
and let it tick over once in a while.
He counts bricks and roof tiles mostly.
They make a neat sum for multiplying.
Not birds. Not twigs or branches.
Once he tried to count snowflakes
but gave up before he was nearly buried
in white. Sometimes it's the number of steps
from the lounge to the bathroom,
growing more each time.
When he is pressed to it, he counts
each breath fluting through his chest.
It's like climbing a ladder he conjures rung by rung
out of the air, amazed
to be still upright, still holding on.

Painting the Lady

He paints her every day,
her belly the perfect canvas.

He doesn't have to ask anymore.
She's always ready. The loaded brush

is a supple thing, sliding over the taut skin.
She takes in colour

with every stroke, blooms while he works.
As he paints his picture, he is painting her.

From the baby, small disturbances,
momentary fault lines on the smooth globe

that is now a blue and white planet,
wreathed in bright oceans, rivers of cloud.

Yesterday was a single malevolent eye,
summoning darkness to keep darkness at bay.

The day before, the skyline
of an imaginary city in skewed perspective.

When he's finished, he lets her see in the mirror,
hoping she will be dazzled again.

She always is, loving them all
and keeps herself uncovered,

until the day is done and it's time
to wash away the colours of this one.

Swimming with Jellyfish

It's only afterwards,
and you've dried off, that you know
what you've been doing,
when the poison begins to burn,
and the scratched nematocysts flare.

Not the brush of a nettle or the sun
but the stroke of these ghosts
you were swimming with,
a world apart from the stained offal
the sea gives up.

In the water they move
like loose balloons,
with a kind of grace, simple as breath,
compelled to rise to the surface,
to consume the food of light.

The Hidden Boy

In this picture, there is a hidden boy.
You will have to look closely to see him.

His ghostly outline is faded into a huddle
of gorse bushes, where he crouches,
staring at whatever unfolds, his eyes yellow petals,
his skin a burr of thorns.

He can remain like this for hours,
pleased to be silent as wood or stone,
sustained on the scent of coconut.

The family eating their picnic on the grass
are unaware they are being watched.
Their eyes are fixed on the fine view,
the estuary spread below them.

The boy records everything they do,
the loud food they stuff their faces with,
their incessant, breezy chatter.

When they have gone, leaving their litter,
a vacuum of quiet, he will come out of hiding,
his bones showing only a clear sky,
his mouth clamped tight on a blue tongue.

The Bird Machine

It started with a surge of rustling wings
I mistook for rain, or a gust of wind.
Then the soft thump of a connecting needle,
fuzzy seconds of white noise
before the singing began, a firework fountain,
a concerto of alarms, each metal heart
cutting new lines into my face.

Drawn to the window, I see the gleaming wires,
dead eyes quick with intelligent fire,
a crowd of neighbours gathered round,
the owner helpless, bewildered.
There is nothing he can do.
He cannot find the instruction manual.
I resume my chair, ready to sit the night out.

The Paranoia of Flowers

Rooted to the spot, we notice everything.
The sky is glass and about to break.
Those blown shadows will cut us like a blade
and faraway, clouds as big as the sea are gathering.

We are lit up against the sky
and shiver in this exposure.
What we can look through does not exist until it shatters.
There is nowhere to hide.

On the restless air, we can hear
the panic of moths, their wings hissing like rain.
Each one of us shimmers to be named
but something is always getting nearer.

Whatever it is will surely fall upon us,
swooping down without warning out of the dusk.

Crossing with the Ferryman

His office is this rowing boat, this river,
sleek and swiftly flowing.
With each deft stroke tuning us in,
he wants to know what brought us here.
Our replies go unremembered while a flock of gulls
streams upwards over dark glass.
He's no concern for the sun's insidious rays,
his head bare, nothing on his feet.
The replicating shadow he already carries
is the thing that will unravel him.
This is the last time he'll take us across,
the last two minutes we'll share.
He pulls upstream to catch the current midway,
gliding back to the other side
with no further effort of the oars,
to reach the landing stage with barely a knock.
We take with us only the pressure
of his steadying hand, nothing
that might be counted and weighed.

Called to Fall

They were always on the margins, quiet people
who never made much of a stir.

Nobody missed them. Their absence no more than a subtle
diminution of light in a room,

the sun going behind a white cloud,
nothing to be remarked upon.

They did not leave together, but as usual
made their way alone.

They moved like sleepwalkers,
eyes open, seeing only the line they were to follow,

as though a voice had started up in their heads,
a diode of desire tripped off, directing their steps

to where they were to go,
their designated places, their slots in the air,

solitary as always. They were to stand so still
that it would appear they had stopped breathing,

become stone or bronze,
gazing down on the water, the scattered flowers

of sunlight. This was how they would be captured
before they dropped out of the frame.

No shot of the fall, the splash, the last proof of them.

The Devil's Nursery

Every morning they would usher us in
from the playground where we cowered, trapped
small figures in a shadowy lithograph
bordered with briars and ravens.

Cooing at us, eager to begin,
they said they had never seen
such good children, so sweet they could eat us.
As we sat down, our foreheads cracked like Pavlovas.

The weather they conjured was always bad,
dishrag clouds teeming with fever,
winds with blue faces screaming around corners
to blow us over and how well we would recall
those days when the slow terror of snow
was summoned for all the mothers to cut
straight lines through the white with their wheels.

Always we were urged to draw closer to the fire
kept blazing and unguarded, cracking out sparks.
We feared to move, being wax or wood,
still as puppets until they pulled our strings.

Every afternoon they laid us down to sleep,
each of us parcelled up in single beds,
our eyes reluctant to close while the cut flowers
around the room breathed out a subtle poison.

When the time came, they promised us,
we would all be called.
There would be a place for everyone.
We were such promising material.

Miss Havisham has a Cigarette

Time for another, she decides,
losing count of how many she's had today.

Not that she cares.
For her the joy of lighting up never fades.

Never as good though as the first one she tried,
with its vertiginous louche impact,

a loosening akin to a touch of the vapours,
of falling into a delicious swoon.

It's a habit now, the effect more measured,
a guaranteed silky insouciance.

Having embraced this sweet craving,
she has set all the clocks ticking again.

Around her, stubbed cigarettes accumulate
in the debris of mouldering wedding cake.

She has redefined her world with smoke,
a necessary accoutrement for standing at a window,

veiled in barred light or exposed to the moon,
after a storm, walking the rain washed streets,

catching a glimpse of stardust between broken cloud,
the wind whipping sparks from her cigarette,

or as she is now, looking down at you
along a barrel of exhaled smoke,

daring you to break the cobweb
of discomposure she has blown in your face.

Bijou Sheiling

It's absurd and marvellous, bracketed
where the trail falls away from the moor:
the freshly glossed clapboard, the manicured lawn,
the rockery, and the rotary washing line,
transported lock, stock and barrel
from a des res neighbourhood
in the suburbs. But a quick look is all we're allowed
for the air is a drizzle of midges,
peppering commas of corpses
over our repellent shiny skin.
Back on the moor, the sea breeze sweeps
the midges away, but it's chaos up here,
an exposed land of peat furrows
and purple heather, scything strokes of cloud shadow,
dumped cars dropped like bombs,
a single capsized caravan.
Inside our dream sheiling though
there's order, comfort, armchairs to sink into,
a carpet of thick pile and one wall for sure
sporting a trio of plaster mallards.

At the Fish Museum

The day was all one risen sea,
subsiding in a charcoal wash of heavy rain.
Anywhere open was a haven from this,
even The Fish Museum.
The lady at the desk scanned us thoroughly,
a flicker of green light in her eyes.
She had our measure.
Patent time wasters with no intention
of buying even so much as a postcard.

There were no fish to be seen.
From behind closed doors, we sensed motion,
shadows, the cleaving of water.
Under her frosty regard,
we made a hasty exit, back out into the rain
streaked with fine white lines like fish bones.

Grove of Dead Trees

You keep coming back here
as though to a cemetery for its bleak repose.

Each time wondering
why there are so many in the one place.

They have become their own gravestones,
marking the spot where the imperative

to grow ran out, stripped clean as bone,
snagged with lightning fractures,

the stumps of amputated branches,
exposed as the pillars of a ruined city,

and would a death this slow be a kind
of ecstasy, to fade as the world

spins ever faster around you?
You should stand with them once

instead of pushing on,
wait until darkness floods the ground,

for a cold white moon to appear,
a scattering of barbed stars.

Yellow on Yellow

The day she came here
with the colours,
saying take whatever catches your eye,
that was a good day.

Yellow on yellow
the colours I chose.

Yellow ink on yellow paper,
the best for me.

The words stayed still.
They showed clear.

She's gone now and they tell me:
this must stop.

Yellow on yellow is impossible.
There will be no colours here.

I have to be sensible.
I have to agree.

I keep my colours hidden now,
take them out when I am alone.
The lid of the tin is a mirror.
I see my face in gold.

I will stand my ground.
I will not be told.

Aeolian Bridge and Two Chestnut Pigs

Since you asked,
that melodious keening is not an emanation
from the spirit world but the harmonics of a breeze
played through wire mesh.

Yes, it is nice here, a lovely spot,
sitting on the river bank
just below the bridge, and with the bonus
of an unexpected signal too.

So soothing to watch this slow river flow
as we catch up with texting and chat.

Further up the track, the pigs are waiting for us.
When we meet them, they won't move at first,
giving us a blank stare.

You'll still have time to exclaim how beautiful they are,
such a striking shade of chestnut,
before they give chase.

As we break into a sprint across the moor,
it will come as quite a surprise to discover
how fast pigs can move.

Their intention is to devour every bit of us.
Nothing will remain to show we once were here.
Even our teeth, crunched and swallowed
as easily as cashew nuts.

If they were human they'd set up a kleptocratic regime,
leave only tracts of churned up earth,
rocks and stones, rusting metal, some trees.

The Solace of Cupboards

What it was that brought it about
that first time, he cannot now quite account for.

That day there was nothing untoward,
no crisis of any kind, only the usual pressures,
as telephones shredded the air,
the photocopier churning out
a set of minutes rife with action points.

But the moment came
when he rose from his desk
without a word to anyone,
slipped the cupboard key off its nook
and strode purposefully away.

He sensed the bewilderment
that followed him along the corridor
but that did not deflect him. He went inside,
locking the door to ensure
he would not be interrupted.

The stacked paper gave off no note,
the packs of pens were voiceless.

Someone went by whose clotted breathing
he recognised but otherwise
there was nothing to prevent him
expanding into an infinite dissolve
that was the solace he had been after.

He believes he is the only one
to have fumbled upon this kind of escape
but there are legions like him everywhere,
standing alone for respite in dark places
until they are ready to be seen again.

How to Sleep

As a necessary precondition, avoid the stimulus
of all forms of philosophical enquiry.
No rest will ensue from pondering the unanswerable
far into the night: How can the statement *I am lying*
be both true and not true?
Is there such a thing as Nothing? Don't go there.

Poetry too is contraindicated, every fretful line of it
a restless churning, each beat, each breath
positively designed to make sleep elusive. Leave it alone.

Eat cheese by all means but not so much
that you begin to shine, lost in staring wakefulness.

Resort to the devil's contract of a hypnotic
if you must but do pause to consider
the acute shortage these days
of physicians who will merrily crank out scripts
for you as a matter of course. It's one line
then you're on your own.

Alcohol you may think does the trick,
tucking you up nicely wherever it leads you
but waking is an exquisite mortification.

Counting each breath is highly recommended,
the lull of numerals lapping you into the realm
of the abstract delivers such peace.

But never be tempted to count sheep.
They congregate so alarmingly.

Neither is it advisable to personify sleeplessness
as a white owl swooping down out of the night
to perch on your shoulder.
You will carry it there for the rest of your life.

Assume the foetal position if you wish,
imagining you are floating in amniotic fluid
though be warned your legs will ache
with the impulse to kick.

Lying on your back is often conducive
in which position you should attempt to outstare the dark,
watching the dust of finely ground graphite
blow in from a nearby pencil factory
as you wait for the film show to begin.

Never regard sleep as a white line on the horizon,
the faint boom of breakers calling to you.
It will always remain out of reach.

But if you really are serious about sleep
we strongly recommend you contact
one of our advisers
here at the Department of Soporific Development,
to discover sleep by steering group, by agenda,
through matters arising,
in national priorities relevant to strategies
already developed by local agencies within
a framework informed by clear and measurable targets,
nested within a performance monitoring policy
to absolutely guarantee sleep, and sleep you will,
a sleep that will seep into your days.
Indeed you will never again be fully awake,
taking your place as one more happy somnambulist,
taking your place with us.

Interior Family

Their voices ring out through the wood.
It belongs to them. It is their living room.
Today lichen provides the only splashes of colour.
Otherwise the background is subdued:
arrangements of trees beaded with drops of rain.
The falls are throws of muslin.
Quite superb really. If only there was not
so much to take account of.
Slow down. Don't get in a huff, dear. No, you are.
You're in a terrible huff.
It's all theirs even though other people get in the way
but something could be overlooked
and there is this compulsion
to keep looping back just in case.
All the while a clock is ticking through the light rain.
They are running out of interiors.
Is it too much to ask not to have yet another spoiled day?

A Drunk Man Dances with a Lamppost

He's overwhelmed with sweet silver notes,
music only he can hear,
the still night air, a ceiling of stars,
and no more to say than the lamppost
while they try out who knows
a foxtrot, a quick step, a Viennese waltz.
They are of the same cast, ungainly, rigid,
veering from a dead slump to spells
of freeze-frame lunges and leans.
His hold on the lamppost alone is constant
as he winds down in clockwork spasms,
legs snapping at the knees,
sharp shoes clattering on the pavement.
However long it takes, he'll keep it up
until they get it right,
take to the floor, step out together.

First Night

Not sleepless, it's that both of you
cannot close your eyes to this
unwavering contemplation,
lying side by side, face to face,
the room lit by a white moon.
Around you, the whole place hums,
wired and monitored.
This is where they cut you apart.
You're adrift now, separate,
no longer sharing the same body,
the same blood.
What is beginning is a slow
unravelling, while the heart demands
to never let go.

A Tall Melancholic Man Contemplates
a Pekinese

Oh, most curious this of anything
he has lately seen, shuffling towards him
along the corridor, pausing to sniff the carpet,
then yanking itself to an abrupt halt
to bristle with, it would appear, irritation
or is it the labour of that over-ripened heart
its small body cannot quite contain?

Of late there has been much to regard
through the narrow lens of his exquisite gloom,
but this perambulating gold cushion, tasselled,
with legs bent like a footstool,
flat face not designed for breathing,
boiled eyes beyond expectation most regal
takes the biscuit. It really does.

His melancholy weighs heavy on him today,
his feet large with gloom, expanding like shadows
towards the nose of the Pekinese,
wrinkling now with interest
and for the first time looking up.
The dog can see what the man is enveloped by,
the dark figures that bind him
and is ready to scare away
these demons, tear at their heels,
run them ragged, dispatch them into the abyss,
if only the man would let go.

Sad Cashier

Exposed in her glass cage,
she doesn't care who sees her misery,

how many drooling voyeurs
run their eyes over the contours of it.

She will not unbend for anyone.
The cash you came for is all you'll get.

When she's finished counting,
scoop it up and leave without a backward glance.

As for giving her a smile, don't.
She'll brush it off like a cobweb.

Tomorrow, walking to work beneath an umbrella
drizzled with white words, she'll be fine again.

At the same time, sequestered in your room,
you'll contemplate a wardrobe crammed with darkness,

a bowl of bruised fruit, the floor
scattered with crisp notes, bright coins.

Fear of Snow

How often it has caught me out
with tiny flakes I thought were specks
of polystyrene blowing down the street.

Then before I know it
I've become a patchwork of white holes.
I'm being slowly obliterated.

I know too well its malign accrual,
the drifts that muffle and hide, that bind my feet,
stifle the song in a bird's throat.

There's no escape, as it blows under the door,
through the letter box, darkening the skylight.

And when it closes in, becomes my prison
of white walls, my tomb, I won't rest,

I won't sleep into it, as it slowly presses
the breath out of me with its weight of wet fur.

The Book of Sheep

Seen from faraway, they are stones that move.
Close up they are scholars,
poring over a vast green manuscript,
a book of hours they faithfully scribe,
working in the fine detail,
each blade of grass, each segment of gold leafed light.

Such dazzling illuminations are offset by the sweep
of turning pages, of unsettling shadows,
the days spinning by like a shoal of clouds,
dark acres rolling across,
incessant downpours drenching their labours
with pools of sudden, puzzling depths
until the broken arch of a rainbow is revealed.

The book takes all their lives to consume and ponder,
to revise and recreate. It consumes them
as they crimp away in a daze of interpretation,
dropping stops all over the ground
of their endeavours, lost in a trail of footnotes.

Their absorption is steady. They seldom rest.
But sometimes a head is raised to pause
for a moment of reflection, or to stare
at whatever catches their eye beyond the margin
of their work. There are disputes too,
differences of opinion erupting across the wide air,
dry chuckles of derision, a chorus of dissent,
or even a brief monologue of despair.

Poor scholars, to us it is a miserable devotion
but they seem indifferent to all their sorrows:
hobbling with foot rot or joints stiff as wood;
swollen with bloat; bearing ticks that bloom
like berries; riddled with worms that barber
the ruched intestinal flesh, drawing the life out of them;
knowing no rest from the swarming itch of scab;
the grass staggers fizzing in their brains like sherbert,
a slow explosion of stained glass.

Move towards them and some will shuffle away
with lowered heads, along an invisible tunnel
where they think they cannot be found
but always there are one or two
to be discovered head down in a stream
turning into a slow work of decay. Otherwise,
they remain where they are,
looking at you as if you were an incoming sea,
a final dark wave rolling over them,
an ending they accept, that they cannot change.

Songs for a Wasted Singer

I. Wine Baby

Wine baby floating on a wine dark sea,
washed ashore then out again
in a suitcase for a crib.

Let's leave her in the lost and found
while she's fast asleep,
pretty as the white moon above,
claret stains on her bib.

When she wakes up, she'll be ready
to scream out her lungs,
mouth wide as a megaphone,
a bawling bag of skin.

Better fetch a bottle for her quick
or she'll wake the whole damn town.

Wine baby flying all around the room,
carousing with the angels,
bumping on the ceiling like a loose balloon.

We can't talk her down, no
she won't ever listen,
thinks she's a princess who's lost her crown.

She believes she's unbreakable,
and you know what: she's right.
When she fell out of the window
she landed light as a kitten, no harm done.

Wine baby drifting off into space.
Come back to see us
when you've had enough
of planets and stars and meteor dust.

You can tell us all about it
and if you choose to stay
you'll be made most welcome
and we'll wet your head again.

II. House of No Illusions

I don't know the address.
I just get taken there.
They wait for me outside
and I get in the car

Keep the engine running.
There's no time to waste.
You know what the truth is
when you get to that place.

Your eyes will be opened,
nothing left of your dreams.
Under no illusions,
there's no other release.

Will I see you this time
barefoot on broken glass,
dancing in your white slip?
Do you know the address?

Trying hard not to sleep
so you don't have to wake,
you know what the truth is
when you get to this place.

It's always different
and it's always the same.
You'll be a work of art.
You'll forget your own name.

Your eyes will be opened,
nothing left of your dreams.
Under no illusions
there's no other release.

47

I don't know the address
I just get taken there.
They wait for me outside
and I get in the car.

III. Broken Bottle

I'm on my back, don't touch me.
Flat on my back, I will remain.
Only leave me where I am lying
And you won't hear me complain.

The ground I'm on's a spinning wheel.
There's no way off.
I can't break free.
Get yourself to Bedlam
and you can leave me be.

Broken bottle's what I've become.
No damn use to anyone.
You can throw me out to sea —
it makes no difference to me.
Broken bottle's what I've become.

I'm on my back, going nowhere.
Flat on my back I will stay.
I can't see straight
to chart my course.
I've got no legs to walk away.

Broken bottle's what I've become.
No damn use to anyone.
You can sweep me up tomorrow
with all the filth and sorrow.
Broken bottle's what I've become.

I'm on my back, don't touch me.
Flat on my back, I will remain.
Only leave me where I am lying
And you won't hear me complain.

IV. Soup of Hard Love

I hope you've no objection
if I begin to play:
I'll take your silence as a yes.
I was going to anyway.

You're in the right establishment
for the point you've reached today.
A spoon is all you'll need, my friend,
in terms of cutlery.

So get in line for what there is
a steaming bowl, soup of hard love.
It's all that you can hope for now.
It's all you're going to have.

On today's menu, you will find
a fine dish that's piquant and hot
and what is more, my friend,
it will stretch your pocket not a jot.

I'm too done in to roll a smoke,
can't see straight to wipe my nose
but I'll play this clapped out piano
until the crows are stoned.

So get in line for what there is
a steaming bowl, soup of hard love.
It's all that you can hope for now.
It's all you're going to have.

Soup of Woe

Down here, the odour of last resort awaits you,
scent of damp dog ends gulled from pavements,
body meat marinated in dosshouses, from sleeping rough,
the tang of the soup you're here for.

You've arrived now. Time to throw away any last vestige
of swagger. You've hit the bottom right enough.
You can't have missed the welcome party
blocking the entrance, waving their bottles like clubs.

Time to take your place for a bowl of woe,
of tears and gristle, scraped membrane, old shoe leather.
You've arrived now. It's hit you between the eyes,
what you saw a long way off, waiting across the track

where they left you laid out, leaking,
flat on your back, waiting for the wagon to come round,
spinning on the axis of sweet oblivion,
the moon burning your visage.

That's you, bobbing up again, Jack easy
on your springs, lurching over to the beat-up piano
to plonk yourself down, plugging fingers into the keys
to coax out chords as smooth as smoke,

a melody that catches her attention,
your queen of love, no matter how wrecked she is
men still favour with more than a fleeting glance,
as she graces you with a nod of appreciation.

Seems you haven't lost your touch.
She's dressed to kill in skinny jeans and white high heels,
and you know if the sea was wine she'd drink it,
every drop, every bubble, all that deep green vintage.

So tell me what's that leaking from your nose?
Oh, that, my friend's the soup of woe.
Then take this crumpled note and smooth it out.
Use it wisely and blow.

Ryder Street

On the soundtrack, nothing was missed
of those days, unwinding now in muddy playback.

Throughout the night, the fridge kept
shuddering to life. It was like sharing a room
with a dog that never needed to be walked.

The head of my bed cheek by jowl
with the sole lavatory of the house
as I learned to distinguish
each of my fellow tenant's signature of release.

Heavy rain turning the fire escape into a waterfall,
the hammering of typewriter keys,
the floor littered with crescents and cuticles
of gouged letters, a visitor throwing up in an orange bowl,
the creaking of the broken bed, a craft
to float away on as the river broke through the streets.

The crowd's roar from the stadium lifting the sky,
subsiding into the stale carpet,
where I stood at the wash basin mirror
contemplating another self-portrait,
my face suddenly wider than it used to be.

When she came to rescue me, I was out,
wandering around, telling everyone I met:
my shoes squeak but I'm happy.

Instant Charisma Shoes

As soon as I saw them, I knew
my long search was over.
Even on the shelf they gave off a glow
that spoke to me of assurance, a gilded life.

I'd found them at last, the shoes
to make me the person I'd always dreamed of being.
I'll take them, I said. The assistant beamed.
She knew they were to die for.

Now I am unquenchable, magnetic,
a swiveller of heads. My confidence shines,
buffed to a lustre that dazzles everyone.
I go where my shoes go.

How wonderful to be this free,
to never look failure in the face,
gliding safely along the edge of every abyss,
never to fall, never to be found out.

The Bible Pornographer

Better than a toilet wall, these hotel bibles
in which to scribble all he can dredge up
from a fount of the obscene.

His deeds wait in bedside cabinets, primed
to go off: joke shop explosions,
a cloud of soot in the face of the next guest

seeking comfort in the word of God.
He used to be an angry man
noted for his fiery exits.

Observe him now at breakfast,
completely in control,
delicately tapping his three minute egg.

This way he's anonymous. Blessedly nondescript
in his dark grey suit and crisp white shirt:
untraceable. The last person

you'd suspect of such a thing.
Sometimes he wonders if there are others
he might claim kinship with,

enough to form an esoteric society,
a worshipful order. Every one sullen as fallen angels,
ready to rise up again and be restored to glory.

Post War Playground

The war is over.
The country full of holes.
When the playtime bell rings
the children flood out,
boys and girls partitioned
by a stout fence.
The boys have machine guns,
the girls skipping ropes.
They move in colour, all of them
crazed Meccano birds.
This is where they'll stand later
neatly lined up to be recorded.
It's only happy, smiling faces
the photographer wants to see,
teeth bright with calcium
from the milk that's free
now the war has gone cold.

Mirror Child

She finds mirrors everywhere:
the surfaces of rivers and ponds, a basin of water,
on the lid of a biscuit tin, on spoons,
on the glass of framed photographs,
the contours of a locked piano.

She's a quiet one, they all agree.
You wouldn't know there was a child in the house.
Where she likes to play best is the parlour,
on the clear understanding she touches nothing.
What she does there all that time, they've no idea.

She would tell them if they would listen,
moving inside mirror after mirror,
not with this body that remains,
nameless and exposed, but the other, unfettered one
that one day she will stand beside.

Porcelain Husband

It's small wonder I wrap him up in cotton wool,
his being so what I call delicate.
It's only natural that I worry, always
on the lookout for something not right
with that perfect complexion of his.

He's easy company, no trouble at all
and always ready with a smile.

I should be thankful I know,
but sometimes I find myself dreaming
of what it would be like to dance in his arms
just the once. He's such neat feet, they'd
light up I'm sure any ballroom floor.

But he's never been one for going out.
He likes to sit enjoying his own company,
in front of the TV, or just watching dust
fall through sunlight. One day I expect
I'll find him broken, on his back,

and that will be that, his eyes that never close,
even when he's asleep, staring up at me.

The Devil's Playmate

Up here, I could be on a plane
cruising high above the clouds,
glass walls on every side,
the same blue abstract to view.
My life is what he promised me:
nothing to do but be beautiful.

The night he singled me out
calling me sweet names,
knowing I would bend, succumb,
was the last night before he set me up
or this swaying pinnacle
above the seasons, the news on the ground.

He takes good care of me.
Anytime I need to leave, I'm free to go,
he's told me many times.
That everything he says is a lie
he makes no secret of and I always
have the window to prove my wings.

Spitting Daisies

Those two up there, spitting daisies
from the fourth floor, cannot hide
their pleasure as each tiny flower
explodes in a precise burst of petals
on the roofs of cars parked below.
Even more gratifying, a direct hit
on the crown of a rare passing hat
calls forth a cheer, a high five.

They do not see their sole witness,
an old man, reared up next
to his prize sprouts, shaking his fist.
If he could get within an inch of them
he'd give them time to waste,
kettle after kettle of it.
He'd give them spitting daisies.
He'd give them something to spit about.

Waiting to be Found

You cannot touch them yet.

They are more patient than you are;
sustained by no expectations.

They stare ahead, waiting,
faces flickering like flowers in the gloom.

All they have is a sweet humming vacancy
into which they have rocked themselves.

There are so many of them housed here:
locked away, forgotten.

When their time comes, give them your attention,
calling them out, one by one.

Be ready to hold them.

Shush

Almost as soon as I settle down to listen
to Beethoven's String Quartet in F Minor,
The Quartetto Serioso, ready to enter this
delicately garnered space, my daughter

in the next room begins to whistle.
Ludwig's flamboyant progress
is instantly demolished. There is no contest.
For her whistle is absolute now.

It has reached a pinnacle of shrillness,
piercing every corner of the house.
A whistle worthy of a butcher's boy,
it has been years in the making.

The early efforts barely a sound at all,
a jet of breath to blow out birthday candles
or release a shower of dandelion seeds.
Later on the first notes were realised,

stray airs like a piping breeze
a faint ghost of a whistle pursuing me
to which I was commanded to listen.
Now all that practice has created this device

to shatter my flimsy elaborations of peace.
Each time I think it is about to finish,
it strikes up again with renewed vigour.
In my head, I rehearse interventions,

seeing myself rise from my chair,
to ask her please to shush,
to cease. But the truth
is I cannot bring myself to do this

and I know I won't
ever try to stop this unconsidered joy,
this glorious noise
of which she is the instrument.

Seeking Sanctuary at the Salvation Hotel

I'm a skinny man with a fat aura,
the world's my china shop.
This is me, back in the hotel again.
One room's enough to house my gloom,
third floor, overlooking the river,
brown glass for gulls to cut diamond lines upon,
a sepia sky, harpstringed with a suicide bridge.
I like it here. Nobody I need to speak to.
Nothing of value to break.
A constant hum is in my head
or from somewhere off like heavy traffic
through concrete pillars. I've renewed acquaintance
with the padded lift, punching the faux leather
fondly this time. The formica bathroom suite's
still chipped, and the radiator clanks into life
like signalling apparatus from the age of steam.
The headboard's slumped to the floor
behind the mattress. I couldn't chew enough gum
to fix it back on. All I'm here to do
is listen to the unrelenting fugue
that's playing through me until it comes to a close.
One day it'll grip me for so long, I'll turn to vapour.
I won't knock into anything then,
leave no mark upon a polished surface,
shatter no prized possession. You ll breathe me in.
I'll be a funny taste in your mouth.

Bawling Baby Jesus

After the painting, Nativity, *by Sheila Mullen*

Oh but you're a ball of fury tonight,
little man, won't be hushed, not for anything.

What's wrong we can only guess.
Are there demons tearing you to pieces,
a blade of gripe slicing you through,
a hunger that can't be fed?

You've screamed your mouth
into a little gaping hell hole. You're tangled
in ropes from trying to pull the stars down.
What are we going to do with you?

Shall we put you outside,
leave you hanging from a tree?
What will your father say
to all this racket? You'll wake the whole house.

Oh please, for all our sakes, cry yourself asleep,
be dead to the world, give us peace.

Shadow Child

What has that child been doing again?
Don't tell me: snipping out shadows,
all shapes and sizes, a mess.

No doubt there'll be little silhouettes of us,
with our teeth and happiness obliterated.
Are we never to be spared this?

She hides herself away for hour after hour
while we wait for her to go off like a siren,
to publish herself, to show us up.

And that stare she gives me,
fixed on something beyond my shoulder.
What is it she's so fascinated by?

As for how many times a day she washes herself
I lose count, the plughole clogged with shadows
I have to steel myself to deal with.

What has she to wash away?
It is beyond anything. If she only knew
what she was doing to us.

This obsession with shadows.
She finds them no matter how well hidden.
She flaunts them in our faces.

Worse than that, the journal she keeps
fat with shadows, sticking to every page.
To think her hands did this.

Her hands looming with shadows,
that flutter all around me
and will not be brushed away.

Hurry Along There

The train to Perdition is packed with sinners,
all of them giddy at the prospect,
already savouring the hurdy gurdy music
of a real good time.

The aisles are jammed with bags and cases,
beachballs, windbreakers, buckets and spades,
the odd fickle kite.

Oh, they can't get there quick enough.
When the whistle blows,
how they stomp and cheer.

Watching all this commotion, the righteous,
on the opposite platform,
are still waiting for their train
which is already woefully late.

No Cargo

He's berthed at last, hauled to rest.
This small vessel holds him secure, with no cargo
but himself. He's dressed for a funeral in his best suit,
draped in white taffeta. His face has grown so small,
the colour of amber wax, withered apple.
Give him a kiss now.
Say goodbye. He won't say it back.
The engine of his voice has gone, gone for good.
A candle blooms in a corner of the room.
Soft music is playing: a slow, incoming tide.

Oh

It's my turn to walk with the baby,
holding her in my arms, up and down the corridor,
circling each room, to get her to settle,
though I know she will not.

Everything is fine as long as the two of us stay
locked together. But I know as soon
as I put her down in her cot
she will go off again like an alarm.

She as awake as it is possible to be
and wants to be shown all that I can put before her.
That a packet of teabags emptied out
makes a family of slumbering mice

and a light switch can blow the darkness from a room.
I show her the night is a flat black screen,
that pellets of rain are hitting the window,
rolling down it in clear veins.

She wriggles forward, one closed hand
blossoming into blunt fingers,
to touch the glass, greet it with that one syllable, oh —
her only word. And this is how we are seen

by whoever is watching us:
a thief drawing away into the night; an angel gliding by;
a satellite spinning through space,
through the darkness we so faintly pierce.

Henry James Riding a Bicycle

The fields of the sea are cobalt today
and to his eye aligned higher than the land,
the green contours of which he follows,
feeding on the unexpressed pleasure
of being perched, held aloft, in this way,
so many glimpsed instances to notice and gather,
scatterings of wild flowers, hedgerows
bristling with insects and small birds,
and above all a clear blue sky
where larks have elected to erase themselves.
All gradients so far he's pleased to note
have made no acute demands upon him,
his breath barely fluttering on the butterfly air.
Such satisfactions there are in the simple labour
of this dogged propulsion, the wheels spinning
with a fine vibration, something between a tick
and a purr, on this good grey road.
The thought one must never entertain
is to wonder how this is possible at all,
this precarious but heady alignment.
The slightest intimation of a wobble
must be resolutely suppressed. What is called for
is to perpetuate all that is vertical,
all that's most wonderfully perpendicular.